WORLD MISSION:

12 studies on the biblical basis

Ada & Ginny Lum

InterVarsity Press
Downers Grove
Illinois 60515

© 1976 by Inter-Varsity
Christian Fellowship of the
United States of America

All rights reserved.
No part of this book may be
reproduced in any form
without written permission from
InterVarsity Press.

InterVarsity Press is the book
publishing division of Inter-Varsity
Christian Fellowship, a student
movement active on campus
at hundreds of universities,
colleges and schools of nursing.
For information about local and
regional activities, write
IVCF, 233 Langdon St.,
Madison, WI 53703.
Portions of the Introduction have
been adapted from material by
Ada Lum in The Evangelistic
Bible Study Compendium,
by IFES Far East, and
used by permission.

ISBN 0-87784-459-3
Library of Congress Catalog
Card Number: 76-21461

Printed in the United
States of America

Contents

1. **God Reveals His Purpose for Humanity**   10
   Genesis 1:1—2:3
2. **Humanity Rebels against Its Creator**   15
   Genesis 3:1-24
3. **Abraham: Father of a Servant Nation**   20
   Genesis 12:1-20; 22:1-19
4. **Isaiah: The Vision of God's Kingdom**   25
   Isaiah 11:1-11
5. **Jonah: A Reluctant Missionary**   30
   Jonah 3—4
6. **Jesus Ushers in the Kingdom**   35
   Mark 1:14-20; Luke 4:16-44
7. **Jesus Trains His Followers for World Mission**   40
   Luke 9:57—10:12
8. **Jesus Faces Death for the World**   45
   John 12:20-36
9. **Jesus' Resurrection Declares His Lordship**   51
   Matthew 28:1-20
10. **The Apostles and World Mission**   56
    Acts 10:1-48
11. **An Apostolic Team in Action**   61
    Acts 17:1-15; 1 Thessalonians 1:1—2:8
12. **The Return of the King**   67
    Revelation 21:1-8; 22:6-21

Introduction

How often have you heard a talk or sermon on missions that pointed only to the Great Commission, "Go ye into all the world . . . ," as a basis for the missionary enterprise? Since this passage is emphasized so much to the exclusion of the rest of the Bible, it can seem that Jesus' last command to his disciples was just an afterthought, "Oops! Before I go, I'd better tell them what to do now."

Though this may be an exaggeration, we fall into many misimpressions about God's world mission because we do not know the breadth and depth of material found in the Scriptures on this crucial topic. Like ancient Israel, we fail to see God's purpose and activity outside the narrow confines of our own home territory. Israel was not sure that the Lord really did reign over the other nations. Their concept of mission, therefore, was greatly affected by their concept of God.

Today we wonder, is God big enough to be concerned for the whole world? Did he have enough foresight to plan for all time? Our concepts of God and his purposes for the whole world also affect our concepts of ourselves and our purpose in the world. Obviously a correct understanding of each is needed if we are to be the people God wants us to be and to do the things he wants us to do throughout the world.

Thus this series of studies begins with a discussion of God in Genesis 1 and what that can tell us of all he intends for us and for the whole world. His purpose is spelled out further throughout the Old Testament. We could study the praises of the psalms. ("The earth is the LORD's and the fullness thereof, the world and those who dwell therein" —Ps. 24:1; "Say among the nations, 'The LORD reigns! Yea, the world is established, it shall never be moved; he will judge the peoples with equity' "—Ps. 96:10.) We could study the judgments of the prophets. ("The LORD will roar from on high, and from his holy habitation utter his voice; he will roar mightily against his fold, and shout, like those who tread grapes, against all the inhabitants of the earth"—Jer. 25:30; "Let the nations bestir themselves, and come up to the valley of Jehoshaphat; for there I will sit to judge all the nations round about"—Joel 3:12.) Space does not permit this.

We have tried, however, to select a few of the many passages throughout Scripture which are representative of God's purpose for the whole earth. You will see his promise to all nations through Abraham. You will get a glimpse of his kingdom in Isaiah and a fuller view in Christ's own life. And you will see, hopefully and prayerfully, more clearly where God wants each of us in his plan for the whole world.

These studies can be used by individuals and groups. If a group uses them, ideally each member will have a copy of this guide and will work through each study on his own before the group gathers for the discussion. The Revised Standard Version of the Bible was used in preparing this guide, and while it is not essential for study, it or another modern version is recommended.

A Word to Group Leaders

You will find, if you are leading a group discussion, that there are two ways you will need to prepare: prayer and study. First, pray for yourself. Then study the passage to hear God speak to you. Don't think about the group. Reflect on the implications of God's Word for yourself. Stay with the passage until you feel at home with it.

Now study the passage again, but with the group in

mind. Jot down the main points that are especially relevant to that group. Pray for sensitivity here. Have a mental "dress rehearsal." What will you do to encourage a relaxed and open atmosphere so people feel free to think with each other, ask questions that really bother them and share their real selves? Pray for the members of your group.

This book, especially if you are the only one with a copy, is a guide for your preparation, not a mechanical pattern to follow in your group. But be both flexible and firm. That is, don't let your flexibility become purposeless, nor your firmness become rigid.

If you are well-prepared, both in study and in prayer, then you will have the freedom to be open to the Spirit's guidance during the progress of the group study/discussion. You will be more relaxed in your leadership, especially able to listen well. You can spontaneously ask questions not in the guide that the group needs in order to search the text more carefully and to think about its meaning more deeply.

The context should always be used to introduce the passage for it gives historical continuity and affects the interpretation of the text. However, you should also have your own brief, "local" introduction before this to show the relevance of the study and to help members anticipate it.

Notes on the text are for clarifying technical, vague or even overfamiliar words and phrases. The discussion may not need all these explanations, but even if it should, keep them simple.

The subdivisions are intended to help you remember the structure of the text and the progress of the main ideas toward the climax/conclusion. Then you need not be glued to your notes during the discussion.

Questions should sometimes be reworded to sound like you and to reach the group at its level. But be careful not to lose their intent nor general order. In your own preparation do not simply answer them in a vague, general way.

Keep looking for more and more implications. Keep asking yourself, What else can I find here? This, more than anything else, will help you feel confident about encouraging others to probe the text and to make their own discoveries.

As you prepare, visualize the group discussion in order to anticipate possible responses to your questions. Keep asking yourself, How will the members probably respond to this? This will show you how to adapt or reword certain questions. It can also help you know what further questions to ask—or not to ask.

Always there are several reflection/application questions at the end of each study. But you may have time in the group to discuss only one. If you think through all of them, you will be prepared to know which one the group is ready for as you see the actual progression of the discussion.

During the study itself, there are a few basic things you will want to keep in mind. First, the aim of any Bible study should be to gain fresh knowledge and insight about God in a life-changing way.

Second, your basic responsibility as leader is to enable the members of the group to discover for themselves what the Bible says and means. Therefore, your main tools are questions (and good ears!). Wise use of them will enable the members to study together. You coordinate the discussion by linking members' contributions and periodically summarizing. But be careful not to make yourself the constant point of reference or the final authority. Seek also not only to cover the text but to promote friendly interaction. (Some people are not used to learning by group discussion or to any kind of Bible study. Do not force participation. It will come when God's Word moves them.)

Most questions in this guide are designed to call forth several possible answers from the text or viewpoints of judgment. This makes for more provoking discussion. So, for healthy group interaction, encourage maximum participation. Every contribution whether "big" or "small" can help to modify the members' thinking so that together you are all pushing into further truth. So, as leader you can help the group probe more deeply by not merely accepting the first answer given, but by asking, "What else do you see here?" or "Perhaps someone has another viewpoint."

Lastly, watch your time so that you spend the last fourth on practical application. This means you may not be able to linger on earlier questions as long as you or some members would like. In such a case you might suggest that there can be better understanding of that point when the group has an overall understanding of the passage. Sometimes, too, questions can be omitted because the group has naturally covered that part.

To summarize, a wise leader will:
- ☐ create an honest, open atmosphere of acceptance;
- ☐ encourage free expression and questions, usually referring them back to the group;
- ☐ give people time to think;
- ☐ encourage members to check their opinions with the biblical record;
- ☐ seek several viewpoints on significant questions;
- ☐ distinguish between general knowledge, opinion and biblical fact;
- ☐ summarize briefly;
- ☐ end on time.

In other words he will:
- ☐ not be dogmatic or argumentative;
- ☐ not do all the talking;
- ☐ not answer his own questions;
- ☐ not depend on personal experience and subjective opinions for authority;
- ☐ not be satisfied with only the first answer or viewpoint expressed;
- ☐ not be afraid of differences in viewpoints or of tactfully challenging superficial responses;
- ☐ nor get off the subject!

A Word to Group Members

Members have responsibilities, too! The basic task of the members in any study/discussion is to search the text and to think cooperatively about what it really says and means. So come with expectancy to learn and discover new insights. Come with humility to listen and share with others. Come with courage to change and be changed. The more you participate, the more you'll enjoy the time.

Maximum participation is desirable. But much talking does not always mean progression in pushing forward together. A profitable discussion is one which is reflective, where people *listen* carefully to others, *think* through what they mean *and then link* their contributions to others and their ideas about the text.

You link with others and their ideas when you expand, modify, question, correct (tactfully!), illustrate or reinforce what they have said. You also contribute when you introduce a fresh viewpoint and when you ask relevant questions for information, clarification or deeper probing. You can sometimes help someone reword a difficult or awkward question. Develop sensitivity to others and help relieve tensions that may arise.

A good discussion moves along when members are saying, "I see something else here" or "I don't quite understand that point. Could you rephrase it?" or "I wonder if perhaps the writer could have another meaning" or "What puzzles me about this verse is. . . ."

You can sometimes help the leader by rewording a difficult or awkward question. Developing sensitivity to others and helping relieve tensions that may arise in the group are other contributions you can make to help the study be the best one possible.

1 God Reveals His Purpose for Humanity

[Genesis 1:1—2:3]

In the beginning God created the heavens and the earth. . . . So God created man in his own image. . . . And God saw everything that he had made, and behold, it was very good. Genesis 1:1, 27, 31

    The Bible sometimes uses "the language of appearance." This is especially so in the following passage. The poet, considering what appears to the human eye, does not describe *less accurately* than the scientist who uses technical terms. Instead, the poet describes *differently* from the scientist. So the focus is not on scientific explanations.

    Observe what the text says. Keep asking, What is the writer trying to communicate to his readers? What is his purpose? (For example, the fact that he mentions God thirty-five times in as many verses indicates his central concerns.) In this way you will discover *why* (though not primarily *how*) God created the world and the human race.

Notes on the Text

1:1 *created:* In the Old Testament the subject of the verb *bārā* (the Hebrew word translated *created*) is always God. Its uses in verses 1, 21, 27 mark three great beginnings:

(1) creation out of nothing, (2) creation of animal life and (3) creation of the human race.

1:26 *image, likeness:* Not accidental or incidental but intentional similarity.

1:26 *us:* This Hebraism revealed later in Scripture as the Triune God, indicates that unity is plural.

A Look at God and Creation [*Gen. 1:1-31*]

1. What comes to your mind when you think of God?

_____

_____

2. Read Genesis 1:1-31 checking the notes above. List repeated words and ideas. What is emphasized?

_____

_____

_____

3. What are some of the implications of the phrase, "God saw that it was good"?

_____

_____

4. List all the different verbs where God is the subject. What fundamental ideas about God do you see?

_____

_____

_____

5. What contrasts are there in the passage? What progression, if any, does there appear to be?

_____

_____

_____

From these what else do you learn about God?

_____

Now consider your answer to question 1. After having studied this chapter, how do you think your understanding of God needs to be changed or deepened?

_____

_____

A Closer Look at Humanity [Gen. 1:24-31]
6. Read Genesis 1:24-31. On the sixth day God creates land animals and people. How does the passage indicate these creatures are similar? (Note also Gen. 2:7, 19.)

_____

_____

On the other hand, how are land animals and people said to be dissimilar?

_____

_____

7. What responsibilities does God give to the human race (vv. 26-29)?

_____

What is implied about people and creation by the fact that we have these responsibilities?

_____

_____

What is the relationship between us and our Creator God to be like?

_____

_____

If we indeed are made in God's image, then which of his characteristics should we expect to see in people?

_____

_____

8. Does the passage tell us anything else about humanity?

_____

_____

Which truth about humanity in this passage do you think is most important?

_____

9. Take a few minutes to write in your own words a fresh statement of God's purpose for creating the human race.

_____

_____

_____

God on the Seventh Day [*Gen. 2:1-3*]
10. Read 2:1-3. What picture of God does the writer emphasize in this concluding section?

_____

How does this add to the picture of God in Genesis 1?

_____

_____

Reflection/Application
11. Do you feel differently about different people? Should you? Or should you have the same attitude toward everyone? Give reasons.

_____

_____

Before this study, how would you have defined "human"? How do you disagree if at all, with the Genesis view?

_____

_____

12. We are made in the image of God. As a Christian, in what ways do you reflect—or deflect—God's greatness, his goodness, his glory?

_____

_____

8. How could you summarize God's attitude toward and purposes for humanity?

Reflection/Application
9. What facts about people and God in this passage should motivate Christians to proclaim the good news of Jesus?

10. Sometime this week use this passage to explain to a non-Christian the greatness of human potential intended by God.

3 Abraham: Father of a Servant Nation

[Genesis 12:1-20; 22:1-19]

Now the LORD said to Abram, "Go from your country . . . to the land that I will show you. And I will make of you a great nation. . . . By you all the families of the earth shall bless themselves." Genesis 12:1-3

Genesis 4—11 chronicles the history of human rebellion against God despite his many acts of grace. The events of the great flood in Noah's time and the arrogant tower of Babel point to God's continued judgment and mercy, mercy and judgment.

Around 2000 B.C. God again intervenes. In Ur, the sophisticated capital of the Chaldean Empire, he finds a man who believes in him and his vision for a new world. History and archaeology tell of a civilization highly advanced in many scientific, architectural and aesthetic ways, but utterly corrupt and idolatrous in syncretistic, polytheistic religions in which moon worship is dominant. Into this human darkness God's light comes to that man. History takes a decisive turn—and the rest of the Bible is the record of what happens because of that one man's faith and vision of God.

Notes on the Text

12:1 *Abram:* Meaning "high father"; also note 17:5 where God modifies his name to *Abraham*, "high father of a multitude."

12:1 This call comes to Abraham in Haran, but according to Acts 7:2-4 God had initially called him in Ur. God may also have called his father Terah ("delay"), but in vain. See Genesis 11:31-32.

12:2-3 This promise is really a reinstitution of God's original world order. It becomes a covenant in 17:1-8 which is so important that God repeats it in 18:18; 22:17-18; 26:3-4; 28:3-4, 12-14; 35:11.

12:6 *the place at Shechem:* Note Bethel in verse 8. Both locations were apparently ancient idolatrous shrines in pagan strongholds.

12:13 *my sister:* Technically true (see 20:12); the people of Haran highly esteemed wife-sister relationships, but Abraham obviously intended to deceive the Egyptians; Sarah was a great beauty at sixty-five (a new mother at ninety)!

22:4 *the third day:* The three-day journey covered fifty miles between the coastal Gerar (20:1) and inland Moriah (22:2).

22:8 *provide:* From the verb "to see"; hence, "God will see to it" is an apt translation. Also note verse 14.

The Starting Point [Gen. 12:1-3]

1. First read Genesis 12:1-20 checking the notes. Considering all the human factors that work against God's call to Abraham in his cultural setting and personal situation (also note 11:30 and 12:4), what struggles does he probably have to go through?

_____

_____

Why might this call be terrifying? attractive?

2. God gives Abraham only one, yet profoundly comprehensive, command. He also makes several promises. What are they?

Put yourself in Abraham's sandals. How do you visualize the concrete possibilities of each succeeding promise? What is the most mind boggling? Why?

The Long Road of Testing [*Gen. 12:4-20*]
3. The faith and vision of Abraham and Sarah are progressively challenged for the next twenty-five years until Isaac is finally born to Sarah, who is far past the age of childbearing. Genesis 12—20 records this spiritual pilgrimage as alternating experiences of human falterings and growing obedience. Look at 12:4-20. When does Abraham falter in his faith in God and his promises?

What kind of character does this reveal in Abraham?

Where do you find instances of growing obedience to God?

Test of a Lifetime [Gen. 22:1-19]

4. Read 22:1-19 checking the notes. From the start we know the outcome of this highly dramatic event, but Abraham does not know it until the very end. What may he have been thinking and feeling during the night after receiving God's shocking command and on the three-day journey to the mountain?

By what phrases does the writer bring out the warm father/son relation?

5. Why is God testing Abraham so severely?

What kind of relationship between them does the whole event imply?

What does God want for Abraham? and subsequently for the whole world?

Reflection/Application

6. In this whole incident think of what is at stake for God, for Abraham, for the world! The vision God gives to Abraham goes beyond himself as an individual to a servant nation blessing the whole world. In what ways does God expect us as his church to be servants to the world?

_____

_____

7. What makes it difficult for you to be more actively involved in God's world mission?

_____

_____

Which aspect of Abraham's example of faith can help you?

_____

8. "God will see to it!" What are the specific needs for which you can believe that "God will see to it"?

_____

_____

4
Isaiah: The Vision of God's Kingdom

[Isaiah 11:1-11]

In that day the root of Jesse shall stand as an ensign to the peoples; him shall the nations seek, and his dwellings shall be glorious. Isaiah 11:10

Over a thousand years have passed between Abraham and Isaiah. During this time the Jewish nation was born, grew up, became a monarchy (against God's will), secured its borders, then became a pawn of powerful neighbors. It also split into two kingdoms.

The northern kingdom of Israel and the kingdom of Syria have allied themselves against the threat of Assyrian domination. They seek to engage Judah's (the southern kingdom's) support—by force if necessary (7:1-9). Instead of turning to God for help, Judah's king Ahaz decides to seek Assyria's aid against Israel and Syria. The result is that Judah becomes Assyria's satellite. The prophet Isaiah warns against such a course of action and urges Judah to rely on God.

In chapter ten Isaiah foretells the judgment coming from God to the arrogant Assyria. This brutal, once powerful nation is pictured as a devastated forest. But God will also judge his chosen people (seen here as a tree felled but not dead) for their unfaithfulness.

Notes on the Text
11:1 *shoot:* See also Isaiah 11:10 and Revelation 22:16.
11:1 *stump of Jesse:* Jesse is King David's father and also Jesus' ancestor.
11:2-3 *fear:* Obedience that results from reverence for God's authority.
11:4 *rod:* An instrument of discipline or punishment.
11:5 *girdle:* A ceremonial sash worn by high priests.
11:10 *ensign:* In military use, a flag or banner indicating nationality.

Signs of Hope [Is. 11:1-11]
1. This passage is one of several well-known messianic prophecies which Jesus would begin to fulfill 750 years later and which he will complete upon his return. But Isaiah is also describing the more imminent time of destruction when the remnant of God's people will be tempted to despair.

Read Isaiah 11:1-11 checking the notes. Write down the signs of hope that Isaiah gives Judah.

_____

_____

_____

_____

According to Isaiah, what is the basic source of the hope he describes?

_____

The Character of the Messiah [Is. 11:1-3a]
2. Look again at verses 1-3a. The Messiah has royal ancestry, but what is the more important and basic qualification that suits him for his role?

What gifts of leadership grow out of this?

3. How is the Messiah's relationship to God described?

Could you describe your relationship with God in this way? Why or why not?

4. Which gift or gifts of leadership from the Messiah's model do you need most in your fellowship group and why?

The Character of the Messiah's Reign [Is. 11:3b-5]
5. Read over verses 1-5. The qualities of the Messiah's rule (vv. 3b-5) arise from the qualities of his character (vv. 1-3a). List the qualities of his rule.

6. Considering the bases and methods the Messiah uses for judgment, what differences are implied between his rule and that of worldly leaders?

Keep in mind the qualities of the Messiah's rule as you read the next section on the results of his rule.

The Results of His Reign [Is. 11:6-11]

7. Now reread 11:6-11. Isaiah describes the results of the Messiah's rule. In a word or phrase give a title to the picture he draws.

8. Into what two categories do the animals fall?

What has happened to them?

What other changed relationships does Isaiah talk about in verses 8-11?

What has brought about this harmonious living?

Imagine this idyllic scene. What pictures of your hope of reconciled relationships, character transformation or renewed trust in others would you add?

9. What picture of God do the last three verses suggest? What is the scope of this picture?

Reflection/Application
10. God's kingdom will be perfected when the Lord Jesus comes again. Meanwhile what model does he provide for our social responsibilities in the world?

What can and should we be doing for the poor? the weak? the wicked?

5
Jonah: A Reluctant Missionary

[Jonah 3—4]

Then the word of the LORD came to Jonah a second time, saying, "Arise, go to Nineveh, that great city, and proclaim to it the message that I tell you." Jonah 3:1-2

    The nation of Israel, chosen by God to be his servants to the rest of the world, lapsed more and more into unfaithfulness. To recall and remind them of their unique position, God often had to bring judgment through foreign enemies. He warned them through his prophets. But even these special spokesmen sometimes had problems understanding that God's concern was for the whole world and not only for the Jews. The story of Jonah clearly reveals this problem.

    The early part of Jonah is better known than the latter because of its big fish story! The facts are straightforward: God calls Jonah to preach his message to non-Jewish Nineveh because of its great wickedness; instead of obeying God, Jonah defiantly flees in the opposite direction to Tarshish (probably in Spain); to bring Jonah to his obedient senses, God uses a great wind, a great panic and a great fish.

Notes on the Text

3:3 *Nineveh:* The great capital of the powerful, heathen Assyrian empire which, in its pursuit of world domination, constantly and brutally harassed Israel.

3:6 *sackcloth and ashes:* A sign of mourning for the dead, or for personal or national disaster, or for penitence of sins.

3:7-8 Note 4:11 for the inclusion of animals in repentance and compassion!

3:10 *God repented:* This is an anthropomorphism (describing God's actions or attitudes in human terms), meaning a change of mind. Whenever the Bible speaks of God repenting, it is directly related to people's repentance or absolute refusal to repent. See also Joel 2:13-14 and Jeremiah 18:5-10.

4:6 *plant:* Probably the thick- and large-leafed castor oil plant.

4:11 *do not know:* Nineveh was ignorant of God's law (as the Jews were not).

Jonah and His Gentile Enemies [Jon. 3]

1. Read chapter 3 checking the notes as you go. Remembering the relationship the Ninevites had with Israel, how much sympathy do you suppose Jonah has for the city?

Then how can he be so powerful and effective in his preaching to them? What outcome might he be expecting from God?

---

2. Repentance is rare today, even though there is much evangelism. Jesus Christ made it a high priority in his evangelism. What does this passage teach us about the nature of genuine repentance?

What does it teach us about God's part in it?

Jonah and His God [Jon. 4]
3. Chapter four is delightful and instructive. It is candid. It is touchingly human. It is humorous. Read the chapter checking the notes. Do you sympathize with Jonah here? Why or why not?

What seems to be his real reason for being angry? (Consider the theological implications of vv. 2-3.)

4. Sum up his qualities as a missionary/evangelist. What are his strong points?

What does he lack?

What do you consider his glaring weakness as a Jew?

5. How does God counsel his pouting prophet?

What primary lesson is he teaching Jonah?

What aspects of God's character come through strongly?

6. The book ends in an interesting (humorous?) way. Perhaps the author also intends the question for his readers: How much of God's compassion do you have? How much are you willing to go to others with his message of repentance and faith in Jesus Christ as Lord?

Reflection/Application
7. Reflect on the kind of God we say we serve. What is he asking us to do for our world today? Who are the "Gentile enemies" God may want us to go to with his message?

Why is it hard to feel compassion for them?

8. In a sense God can get along without our missionary

service. Then why does he pursue us when we evade his commission to us?

_____

_____

9. Powerful preaching without compassion for people—that was Jonah! Let God search your heart, and pray to him to see if you are correct in your grasp of biblical facts but devoid of human feelings for fellow creatures.

6 Jesus Ushers in the Kingdom

[Mark 1:14-20; Luke 4:16-44]

Jesus came into Galilee, preaching the gospel of God, and saying, "The time is fulfilled, and the kingdom of God is at hand; repent, and believe in the gospel." Mark 1:14-15

The Hebrew nation has gone through wars and exile since Jonah's time and is now ruled by the foreign power of Rome. They have long awaited liberation through God's promised Messiah (the Anointed One). In the scenes that follow, Jesus, who has just finished his forty-day test in the wilderness, begins his ministry in his home province of Galilee. Its population is diverse but strongly nationalistic, surrounded by unsympathetic Jews and Gentiles. Thus the Galileans symbolize God's people in bondage (Is. 9:1-2), and it is to them that Jesus first comes.

Notes on the Text
Mark 1:14 *John:* The Baptist had been heralding God's imminent visit.
1:15 This summary is the heart of Jesus' message, the key to his mission.
Luke 4:19 *the acceptable year:* God's chosen era of his favor to man.

4:26 *widow of Zarephath:* A Gentile (1 Kings 17:8-16).
4:27 *Naaman the Syrian:* Another Gentile (2 Kings 5:1-14).

Follow Me [Mk. 1:14-20]
1. Read Mark 1:14-20 checking the notes above. In the summary of his message in verses 14-15, observe Jesus' deep sense of having a mission to fulfill. What has God done?

_____

What is man's response to be?

_____

2. Looking at verses 16-20, what do you suppose the four businessmen see and feel about Jesus that makes them follow him?

_____

_____

3. What relationship to the four men is Jesus assuming when he calls them?

_____

What changes might he be expecting of them?

_____

_____

The Spirit of the Lord Is Upon Me [Lk. 4:16-30]
4. Now read Luke 4:16-30 checking the above notes as you go. How does Jesus begin to reveal that he is God's Messiah?

_____

What are the initial reactions to his claim?

Why does the response change to violence?

I Must Preach the Good News [Lk. 4:31-44]

5. Read Luke 4:31-44. This is a typical twenty-four hour day in Jesus' ministry. List different people, times and places.

In what different ways does Jesus proclaim and demonstrate the gospel?

What is his attitude to different human needs?

When is Jesus stern? When is he compassionate?

6. How does what God sends Jesus to do in verses 18-19 compare with what he actually does in verses 31-44?

If Jesus is ushering in the kingdom of God, what are some of its characteristics?

I Was Sent for This Purpose [Lk. 4:16-44]
7. Look again at verses 42-44. What personal discipline do you observe in Jesus' life?

Why do you suppose this is noted just before his announcement of verses 43-44?

8. Imagine yourself as one of Jesus' first four followers, an active observer moving with him throughout Galilee and Judea. What might be your thoughts, feelings and questions about his identity and the messianic mission he claims?

9. What do you consider Jesus' most outstanding characteristic seen in these opening events? Where do you see it most clearly?

_____

_____

Reflection/Application
10. We have been considering what Jesus says his life's mission is and how he began to fulfill it. Take time to write out a brief statement of your life's mission.

_____

_____

_____

_____

Now that you've written it down, does this seem like a worthwhile goal? How does it compare with Jesus' mission?

_____

_____

Think back to God's original purposes in creating the human race and to what he intends his kingdom to be. How can you bring your life's goals more in line with these two things?

_____

_____

_____

7 Jesus Trains His Followers for World Mission

[Luke 9:57—10:12]

After this the Lord appointed seventy others, and sent them on ahead of him, two by two.... And he said to them, "The harvest is plentiful, but the laborers are few." Luke 10:1-2

Jesus' earthly ministry is coming to a close. He continues to prepare his disciples for his suffering and death. The enthusiastic crowd grows, still misunderstanding his intents, still expecting him to enter Jerusalem as their political Messiah. Their ideas of Jesus Christ and their motives for following him vary as the first part of our passage shows.

Notes on the Text
9:58 *Son of man:* Jesus' favorite title for himself as the Messiah, at once man and eternal King. See Daniel 7:13-14.
9:60 *dead to bury the dead:* It is uncertain which Oriental tradition is being referred to here—the time-consuming funeral responsibilities falling on the eldest son or his obligation to remain at home to fulfill his father's wishes. Either case means delay.
10:6 *son of peace:* A man characterized by peace.

10:11 *wipe off against you:* Symbol for cutting off a relationship.
10:12 *Sodom:* Proverbial for God's judgment on wickedness.

Candidates for Discipleship [Lk. 9:57-62]
1. Jesus ministered to people wherever he met them. Now we see him talking to three men, challenging them to think more deeply about what they are saying.

Read Luke 9:57-62 checking the notes. Study the condensed conversations Jesus has with each of the three men. What picture do you have of each one?

_____

_____

_____

What do they have in common?

_____

_____

How do they differ?

_____

_____

2. How much do you think the first man had considered the deeper implications of saying "I will follow you wherever you go"?

_____

By examining Jesus' response to him, what can we know about the man's personal expectations?

_____

3. Jesus' answers to the other men also show their superficial understanding of what it means to follow him. What meanings for *follow* do you think they had in mind?

What is lacking in each man's understanding?

Jesus' Mission for the Seventy [Lk. 10:1-12]
4. Read 10:1-12 checking the above notes. Having defined discipleship more thoroughly, Jesus appoints seventy men to precede him into every town. An atmosphere of crisis prevails. What is the urgency? How does Christ express it?

Why is the analogy of the harvest an apt one?

5. Compare Jesus' challenge to the three would-be followers with the instructions to the seventy men. What expectations does Jesus have for both groups?

6. Jesus set down rigorous principles for his first missionaries. What requirements does he demand of them?

_____

_____

Why do you think Jesus includes the practical instructions?

_____

_____

7. What connection do you see between being a follower of Jesus and being a missionary?

_____

_____

_____

Reflection/Application
8. In which group do you see yourself in your readiness to follow the Lord Jesus—the three or the seventy? What are your reasons?

_____

_____

What qualities do you share with the three would-be followers?

_____

Do you feel you are ready to be part of the seventy? Why or why not?

_____

9. Considering the goals, the method and the message of the first missionaries, what things, if any, have changed for twentieth-century missionaries?

_____

Discuss the universal and timeless principles for missionaries of the Lord Jesus.

_____

10. Write a set of instructions for modern-day missionaries based on the Lord's principles. Share them in your group.

_____

_____

_____

_____

_____

8 Jesus Faces Death for the World

[John 12:20-36]

"And I, when I am lifted up from the earth, will draw all men to myself." John 12:32

In this chapter John ends his account of Jesus' public self-revelation. The Jews have previously been exposed to this revelation. Great crowds still follow him having heard of his raising Lazarus from death. Some sincerely believe, but the nation's leaders reject him. He comes to worship at the feast in the Jerusalem temple where he delivers his last public discourse. Among the worshipers are people whose background and culture are totally different from the Jews'.

Notes on the Text
12:20 *feast:* Passover is a major Jewish feast in early spring observing God's miraculous deliverance of the Jewish people's ancestors from Egyptian slavery. See Exodus 12:23-27.
12:20 *Greeks:* Gentile proselytes who, attracted to a monotheistic and a highly ethical religion, followed the Jewish faith and practice short of circumcision and thus short of becoming full proselytes.

12:21 The mention of *Philip* (A Greek name) and *Bethsaida* (a town near some Greek settlements) implies that the Greeks approached him as one sympathetic to non-Jews.

12:23 *the hour has come:* God's appointed time for Jesus' death for the sins of the world. Compare John 12:27, 32; 13:1; 17:1.

12:24 *Truly, truly:* (Greek—*amen, amen.*) Often used by Jesus to stress the importance of what he is about to say.

12:30 *for your sake, not for mine:* The Semitic construction expresses more a comparison than a strict contrast, that is, "more for your sake than mine." As in Jesus' baptism and transfiguration, God's voice was also personal assurance to him.

12:34 *Son of man:* See note on Luke 9:58 in study seven.

Gentiles Seek Jesus [Jn. 12:20-22]
1. Read 12:20-36 checking the notes. The preceding events (12:9-19) have highly charged the atmosphere in Jerusalem. Look at 12:20-22. Everyone is talking about Jesus. What familiar faces do you see in this scene? What new ones?

What attitudes to Jesus are expressed? Sum up each in a word or phrase.

2. Why did the Greeks come to the feast?

What does this indicate about their spiritual aspirations?

Why do you think they want to see Jesus? (Consider the

circumstances and the manner of the Greeks.)

Why do you think they are indirect in their approach to Jesus?

Dying to Live [*Jn. 12:23-26*]
3. John does not say whether or not the Greeks actually have an audience with Jesus. But what subject does Jesus discuss in response to this request? (See also and especially vv. 27, 31-32.)

What link can you see Jesus making between this subject and the Greeks' desire to see him?

4. In your words what is the spiritual principle Jesus conveys through his agricultural metaphor?

What is the historical demonstration of the truth of each phrase in verses 24-25?

5. Now let us see in verses 25-26 how Jesus specifically applies this "dying to live" principle to his followers. In what practical ways might you "love your life" and end up losing it?

In what practical ways might you "hate your life" and end up keeping it?

Do you think Jesus means "serve" and "follow" to be the same or separate activities? Explain.

Consider the sowing of one seed—Jesus' life and death—and their universal, eternal effects. How paradoxical are some of his teachings until we see his life, death and resurrection as a unit!

Dying to Save [Jn. 12:27-36]
6. Read 12:27-36. What is the attitude of Jesus' prayer?

What are the alternatives facing him, and what are the results of each alternative?

Try to imagine the deep struggles of Jesus. What affects you most?

What kind of relationship do you see between Jesus and the Father?

7. Jesus has alluded to his death in response to the Greeks in verses 23-24, 27. Now he explains it to the crowd. What does he say (explicitly and implicitly) about his impending death (vv. 31-33)?

Why doesn't the crowd understand him?

8. What picture does the writer, John, draw of the crowd?

What does Jesus add to this picture (vv. 35-36)?

Reflection/Application

9. Why do people you know fail to grasp the meaning of Christ's death—its implications for them as individuals? its implications for the world?

10. How can Jesus be the example for us to hate our lives that others might also be saved by his death and life?

9 Jesus' Resurrection Declares His Lordship

[Matthew 28:1-20]

"All authority in heaven and on earth has been given to me. Go therefore and make disciples of all nations." Matthew 28:18-19

The Jewish leaders' thirst for Jesus' blood has overruled the Roman governor's vacillating attempts to prevent his execution. So in the worst kind of public humiliation, Jesus has been crucified. The governor has allowed the wealthy Joseph of Arimathea, a secret disciple, to take Jesus' body to lay in his own new tomb. The chief priests and Pharisees, fearing the disciples' theft of the body as a resurrection fraud, take extra precautions to secure the tomb. Only a few socially insignificant women mourn for him.

Notes on the Text
28:1 *after the Sabbath:* Early Sunday morning.
28:7 *Lo, I have told you:* "That is what I had to tell you" (New English Bible).
28:9 *took hold of his feet:* Middle Eastern manner of showing obeisance to royalty.
28:19 *make disciples:* Make continual learners.

Believers and Disbelievers [Mt. 28:1-15]

1. How differently people respond to the same event! As you read about the resurrection in verses 1-15, checking the notes as you go, note all persons and their particular concerns.

Go with the two women to the tomb. What different emotions do they go through?

_____

What evidences could they give to the disciples that Jesus had risen from death?

_____

_____

2. Galilee was the home province of the disciples. Can you suggest why Jesus designates this place to meet him? (Note Mt. 26:32.)

_____

_____

3. Compare the guards' reactions and actions with the women's.

_____

_____

How do you account for the differences?

_____

_____

4. What impact does the resurrection have on the rulers? (Note Mt. 27:62-66.)

_____

Back in Galilee [Mt. 28:16-17]
5. Note verses 16-17. In contrast to the panic in Jerusalem, Jesus quietly meets his disciples on the mountain in Galilee. What are the different reactions the disciples give to Jesus?

How do you explain the mixed responses?

Had you been one of them, would you have doubted or worshiped? Why?

6. Why was this meeting so strategic for Jesus and his disciples?

Jesus Christ's Great Commission [Mt. 28:18-20]
7. Verses 18-20 have commonly been called "The Great Commission." Why do you think this is so?

In verse 18 how does our Lord Jesus lay the groundwork for the actual commission itself?

How well do the disciples understand the Great Commission? What might have been some of their questions?

8. Re-examine verse 19. The Greek grammar has only one command: "Make disciples." All other verbs are participles (modifying verbs). What actions describe disciple making?

What are the essential teachings of Jesus we must share in making disciples?

9. The thought of partnership with Christ in his world mission is staggering! How does the Lord Jesus participate with his disciples in this world task?

What direct link do you see between Jesus' resurrection and the Great Commission he gave to his disciples?

Reflection/Application

10. The Great Commission was given to the disciples as a body of believers. In Acts it is carried out through teamwork. What action should your church or fellowship take in greater obedience to Jesus' Great Commission?

11. Can you imagine carrying out the Great Commission if Jesus had not risen from death? Why would it be an impossible task?

Consider: To believe in the resurrection of Jesus Christ is to obey his Great Commission.

10 The Apostles and World Mission

[Acts 10:1-48]

And Peter opened his mouth and said: "Truly I perceive that God shows no partiality, but in every nation anyone who fears him and does what is right is acceptable to him."
Acts 10:34-35

Acts 1—9 vividly highlights the spectacular birth and equally spectacular early spread of the Christian movement in the world. But the Christian Jews still believe God's salvation is not for the inferior Gentiles despite the original and repeated covenant between God and his people, and despite Jesus' own reinforcement. God has to do something unmistakable to push them into the rest of the world, just as he did with Jonah. Acts 10 is the obvious New Testament counterpart of the book of Jonah.

Notes on the Text
10:1 *Caesarea:* The magnificent seaport metropolis built by the Roman conquerors as their Judean headquarters.
10:1 *centurion of ... the Italian Cohort:* A noncommissioned officer with a captain's responsibility over a century (one hundred men) which was considered the back-

bone of the Roman army; a cohort had ten centuries.
10:2 *devout man:* "God-fearer"; an uncircumcised sympathizer and so not a full proselyte; see *Greeks* in note on John 12:20 in study eight.
10:5 *Joppa:* The Mediterranean seaport for Jerusalem which was thirty-five miles inland; a day's journey from Caesarea.
10:9 *sixth hour:* Noon by Jewish reckoning; a regular prayer time.
10:14 *common or unclean:* Jesus in Mark 7:14ff had explicitly annulled the Jewish food laws based on Leviticus 11.
10:34 *no partiality:* This was revolutionary for Peter!
10:36 *Christ:* Greek for "the Messiah" (Hebrew) or "the Anointed One."
10:42 *ordained ... to be judge:* Peter may have had in mind the vision of the "Son of Man" as judge in Daniel 7:9-14.

Cornelius: The Gentile God-fearer [*Acts 10:1-8, 22-24, 30-33*]
1. Read Acts 10:1-48 checking the notes as you go. By referring to this episode three times, Luke rightfully notes it as a major crossroad in history. Acts 10 is his account, while Acts 11:1-18 is Peter's defense of his actions and Acts 15 is Peter's reference to it in the crucial Jerusalem Council.

From the many facts that Luke records give a character sketch of Cornelius.

_____

_____

_____

What are indications (explicit and implicit) of his seeking God?

How can you tell who among your acquaintances are searching for God?

Peter: The Jewish Missionary/Evangelist [*Acts 10:9-29*]
2. Let's look at Peter in 10:29. Even though most of us are Gentile Christians, try to describe what Peter was going through psychologically.

What do you learn about God by the way he deals with Peter and his Jewish prejudices?

Why does God use so dramatic a method?

Explaining the Gospel [*Acts 10:34-43*]
3. Examine the summary of Peter's sermon in 10:34-43. It is the heart of the gospel. Compared to the six or seven other evangelistic messages in Acts, it lists most comprehensively the basic facts about Jesus of Nazareth. What are these facts in the order Peter gives them?

_____

_____

_____

_____

Why is each one significant in explaining Jesus Christ to non-Christians?

_____

_____

_____

_____

And Gentiles Also! [*Acts 10:44-48*]
4. Acts 10:44-48 is the second of the three times that Luke records that new converts show external evidence of the Holy Spirit. (See also Acts 2:4, 19:6.) Why would God especially give the gift in this instance?

_____

What amazes the Jewish Christians present?

_____

What are the conclusions that Peter draws from this episode?

Reflection/Application

5. Peter and Jonah were representatives of their people. God intends their stories to teach us as his church, not merely as individuals. In what way is our fellowship still narrow and exclusive in missionary and evangelistic outreach?

What specific principles of evangelism in this passage should encourage us to move out more boldly to seekers around us?

Using Peter's outline explain to a seeker this week the significant facts about Jesus Christ that will help him to see why he should become a Christian.

11 An Apostolic Team in Action

[Acts 17:1-15;
1 Thessalonians
1:1—2:8]

"These men who have turned the world upside down have come here also." Acts 17:6

Paul, Silas and Timothy have just left Philippi where a young but tested church has begun to grow. Moving southwest, the team arrives in Thessalonica. The narrative is simple. Look for underlying principles of missionary work. The first letter Paul wrote to Thessalonica soon after he was ousted from that city is also enlightening.

Notes on the Text
17:1 *Thessalonica:* An international trade center in Macedonia (northern Greece) on the famous Ignatian Highway, boasting an excellent harbor.
17:2 *three weeks:* On three successive Sabbath days.
17:3 *the Christ:* See note on Acts 10:36 in study ten.
17:4 *devout Greeks:* Gentile "God-fearers" who followed Judaism's worship and practice short of becoming full proselytes. See notes on John 12:20 in study eight and on Acts 10:2 in study ten.
17:5 *Jason:* Apparently a new convert with whom Paul was staying.

17:10 *Beroea:* a prosperous town fifty-five miles southwest of Thessalonica.

Missionary Strategy [*Acts 17:1-15*]
1. The comparative study of the evangelization of Thessalonica and Beroea could be expanded to include other cities and regions mentioned in Acts. The apostles basically evangelized their world, the Roman Empire, in one generation of thirty-three years. Thessalonica and Beroea typify their missionary work.

First read Acts 17:1-15 checking the notes above. In both cities where do Paul and his teammates go first?

_____

Why is this common sense strategy?

_____

_____

What other similarities do you observe in the ways Paul and his teammates evangelized Thessalonica and Beroea?

_____

What emphases in evangelism do these similarities bring out?

_____

_____

What differences do you observe?

_____

_____

How can you explain the differences?

_____

2. Nearly every city that Paul and the other apostles evangelized was, like Thessalonica, a major city located on a highway or seaport. What other lessons in missionary strategy might this teach us?

_____

_____

Missionary Message [*Acts 17:1-9*]
3. What points about "the Christ" does Paul stress to the Thessalonians?

_____

_____

Why do you think he needs to do this?

_____

_____

Missionary Methods [*Acts 17:1-15; 1 Thess. 1:1–2:8*]
4. What are the verbs describing the different ways the missionary evangelists present their message (Acts 17:2-3, 11)?

_____

How are these mental activities related to the fact that some of them were "persuaded" (v. 4) and "therefore believed" (v. 12)?

_____

_____

Does argument and reasoning have a place in bringing someone to faith? Why or why not?

_____

_____

5. Read 1 Thessalonians 1:1—2:8. What else does Paul say about the way he conducted himself among the Thessalonians?

_____

_____

Where do Paul's example and teaching point out problems you have in evangelism?

_____

_____

Why do you think you are having these difficulties?

_____

_____

What personal disciplines do you need to overcome these difficulties? (See also 1 Thess. 1:4-5; 2:1-8.)

_____

_____

Missionary Results [*Acts 17:1-15; 1 Thess. 1:6-10*]
6. What were the different types of people mentioned in Acts 17 who accepted the gospel message?

_____

Why do you think Luke takes time to mention them?

7. How do multiple conversions and multiple persecutions both show how effective the team's evangelism was?

What lessons do you think Jason and his new fellow believers began to learn about following Jesus Christ? (See also 1 Thess. 1:6-10.)

8. To what degree are you willing to suffer for Jesus' sake in pioneering evangelism?

How might you be called to suffer in the situation you are in now?

Missionary Follow-Through [*Acts 17:1-15; 1 Thess. 1: 1-10*]
9. What are the problems the young Christians face as described or hinted at in Acts 17:4-9, 13-15 and 1 Thessalonians 1:6-10?

In what specific ways did Paul help them continue to grow, as discussed in Acts 17:9-10, 14-15 and 1 Thessalonians 1:1-3, 6-10?

Reflection/Application
10. Which parts of the apostolic missionary work can you directly apply to your campus or community mission? Which are only indirectly applicable? Explain.

11. What is necessary to produce missionaries of the caliber of the apostles?

12 The Return of the King

[Revelation 21:1-8; 22:6-21]

He who testifies to these things says, "Surely I am coming soon." Amen. Come, Lord Jesus! Revelation 22:20

John has been exiled for his faith on Patmos Island in the Aegean Sea. But God continues to speak to his churches through this faithful servant. Jesus Christ in his eternal majestic kingship reveals the historical events leading up to, as well as the consummation of, his new kingdom. In the last vision John sees a magnificent panorama of history's final stage when the old order passes away and the new heaven and earth appear. This is God's ultimate goal of redeemed humanity.

John naturally uses earthly language to describe or convey these spiritual realities for earthly language is the only one we can understand! Therefore, interpret the physical descriptions as symbols remembering that the spiritual reality is always greater than its symbol.

Notes on the Text
21:2 *holy city, new Jerusalem:* The church; signifies continuity of community among believers of the Old and New Covenants. Note 21:10-14; 22:14.

21:2 *bride:* The church, the body of Christ. Note 22:17.
21:6 *Alpha and Omega:* The first and last letters of the Greek alphabet; applied to Jesus Christ as Originator and Completer of all things. See also 1:8, 17; 2:8; 22:13.
21:8 *second death:* Final separation from God. See Matthew 25:41, 46.
22:14 *those who wash their robes:* Those who conquer (6:11 and 21:7).
22:14 *tree of life:* See Genesis 2:9, 3:22-24; Rev. 22:2.
22:16 *root and offspring of David:* Fulfillment of Isaiah 11:1. See study four.
22:16 *bright morning star:* Symbol of a new day.
22:19 *the book of this prophecy:* The book of Revelation.

I Make All Things New [*Rev. 21:1-8*]
1. Read Revelation 21:1-8 checking the notes. Repetition of an idea or phrase indicates importance. List the repeated references to similar ideas that you find in this passage.

_____

_____

_____

_____

What is God's relationship to man like in the new creation?

_____

_____

2. Here in this vivid portrayal of the new creation we can see God's fulfilled purposes for humanity. What different pictures of God do you see?

How does the new creation differ from the one we live in now?

3. What phrases describe those who qualify for life forever in his new world?

Do these phrases describe you? If so, how?

Who do not qualify? For what reasons?

I Am Coming Soon [Rev. *22:6-15, 20*]
4. What do we learn about the Lord Jesus in 22:6-15, 20?

What dominant fact about Jesus Christ is repeated?

What other subjects are linked to each mention of this fact?

How should our Lord's expected return affect your personal living?

Come, Lord Jesus! [Rev. 22:16-21]
5. Besides the two major themes of our Lord's imminent return and its moral implications for his people, there is a third one seen in 22:16-21. What is this theme, begun in verses 6-7, 9b-10 and climaxed in verses 18-19?

Why is the Lord himself stressing this so much?

6. If our Lord has so stressed the certainty of his prophecies, ought not believers also to look to their fulfillment? Note this in verses 17-19. Who combine to urge the Lord Jesus to come back to earth?

_____

Who else is invited to urge his return?

_____

_____

7. What are some of the main truths you have learned about the Lord Jesus, his kingdom and yourself in it during this series of studies?

_____

_____

_____

_____

Have they gripped you so that you can eagerly say as John did, "Come, Lord Jesus"?

_____

_____

Reflection/Application
8. In what ways might the church of today be guilty of adding to or taking away from the prophecy found in Revelation?

_____

9. Superimpose the picture we saw in Isaiah 11 (study four) over 21:3-7. What response to the King of the New World does this stir in you?

10. What remains for the church to do before her Bridegroom, the Lord Jesus, returns? How should she be preparing herself?